My Religion and Me
We are
SIKHS

Philip Blake

W
FRANKLIN WATTS
LONDON•SYDNEY

This edition copyright © Franklin Watts 2015

Franklin Watts
338 Euston Road
London, NW1 3BH

Franklin Watts Australia
Level 17/207 Kent Street
Sydney, NSW 2000

Series designed and created for Franklin Watts by Storeybooks.

Acknowledgements
The Publisher would like to thank Akaalsimran, Amrita, Sehaj and Sunny
as well as the Gurdwara Sahib in Leamington Spa, for their help in producing
this book.

Faith advisor: Gurmeet Kaur Bhatia

Photo credits: © ArkReligion.com / Alamy p19 (top), © World Religions
Photo Library / Alamy P16, 11 and 19 (bottom); Tudor Photography pp
1(bottom), 3(bottom), 6(bottom), 12, 13, 14, 15 and p17.
Additional photographs were supplied by the children featured in the book
which despite their best efforts may not always be of the highest quality.
Every attempt has been made to clear copyright. Should there be any
inadvertent omission please apply to the publisher for rectification.

Dewey number: 294.6

ISBN: 978 1 4451 3890 9

Printed in Malaysia

Franklin Watts is a division of Hachette Children's Books,
an Hachette UK company. www.hachette.co.uk

Note:
The opinions expressed in this book are personal to the children
we talked to and all opinions are subjective and can vary.

Contents

Words in **bold** can be found in the glossary

What is Sikhism?

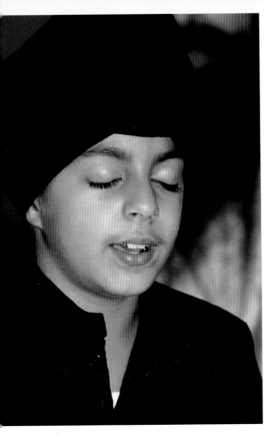

▲ *Sehaj closes his eyes as he meditates on God's name.*

Sikhism is the religion founded by Guru **Nanak** in the Punjab **region** on the borders of India and Pakistan in around 1499. The faith is based on Guru Nanak's teachings and on those of the nine spiritual teachers, or gurus, who followed him.

Beliefs

Sikhs believe in one God. They try to keep God in their hearts and minds always and aim to live well by being honest, working hard and treating all people as equals, whatever religion or social class they belong to. Sikhs try to support and serve others, especially those less fortunate than themselves.

Sunny and his family stand outside the **gurdwara** *where they worship.* ▶

▲ *The Golden Temple at Amritsar, described by Guru Arjan as 'the noblest of all places', is an important place of pilgrimage for Sikhs. This picture is of Akaalsimran and her brother Kirath Dev Singh on a visit to The Golden Temple.*

The sacred book

The teachings of the Sikh gurus are contained in the Sikh sacred book, **Guru Granth Sahib**. The tenth guru, Gobind **Singh**, decided that he would be the last human guru and that when he died, Sikhs should follow the guidance of the book. For this reason, the sacred text has the title and role of a human guru and is treated with the same respect that Sikhs give to Guru Nanak and the other human gurus.

The Sikh community

Sikhs have a very strong sense of **community**. They work hard to help others, both other Sikhs and members of the wider population. If Guru Granth Sahib does not provide an answer to a problem or question, the Sikh community tries to decide the issue together, using the general guidance of Guru Granth Sahib.

5

Sikhism Around the World

Most of the world's Sikhs live in the Punjab where the religion began. Today there are almost 20 million Sikhs in the Punjab. There are also smaller groups of Sikhs living in other parts of the world. Canada has the largest number of Sikhs in the West and there are smaller numbers in countries such as Great Britain, the USA and Australia.

The holiest place for Sikhs is the **Harmandir** Sahib, or Golden Temple, at Amritsar, a city in the Punjab that was founded by Guru Ram Das in 1574. This beautiful building has been attacked by the Sikhs' enemies a number of times over the centuries, but the Sikhs defended it and it remains the home of Guru Granth Sahib and an important centre for Sikhs.

My name is Sehaj Singh. I live with my family in a town called Suwannee in Atlanta, Georgia, USA. I go to a private school. My dad, Gurvinder Singh, is a pharmacist, and my mother, Kamaljit Kaur, is a science teacher at my school. My hobbies are reading, playing basketball and soccer, art and playing video games. My favourite subject at school is maths.

My name is Balraj Singh Bhamrah but most people call me Sunny. I am nine years old and I live in Banbury, England, with my mum, dad, granny and two brothers, Jas and Vik. Jas is 17 and Vik is 15 years old. I like all sports, especially football, tennis and cricket. I also enjoy playing on my Playstation.

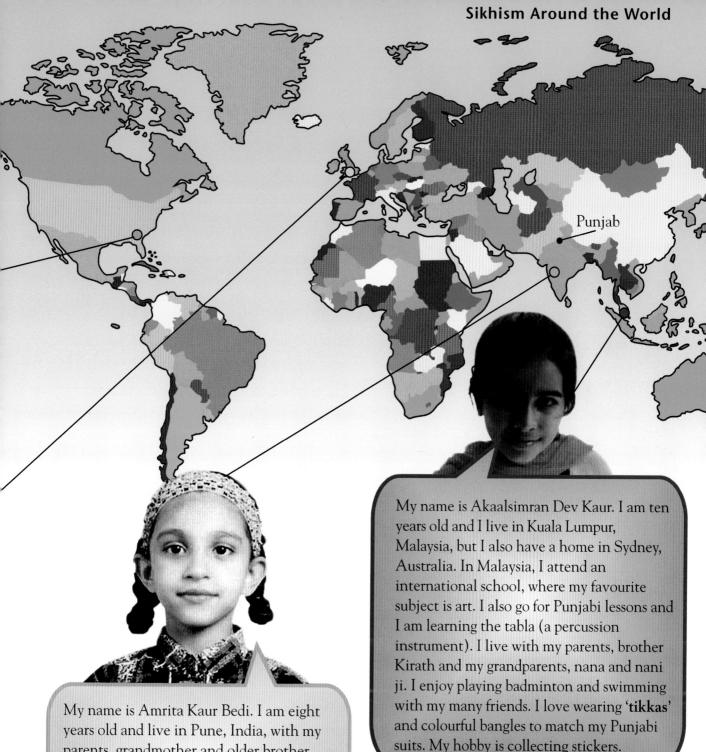

Punjab

My name is Akaalsimran Dev Kaur. I am ten years old and I live in Kuala Lumpur, Malaysia, but I also have a home in Sydney, Australia. In Malaysia, I attend an international school, where my favourite subject is art. I also go for Punjabi lessons and I am learning the tabla (a percussion instrument). I live with my parents, brother Kirath and my grandparents, nana and nani ji. I enjoy playing badminton and swimming with my many friends. I love wearing 'tikkas' and colourful bangles to match my Punjabi suits. My hobby is collecting stickers.

My name is Amrita Kaur Bedi. I am eight years old and live in Pune, India, with my parents, grandmother and older brother. My hobbies are singing, swimming, biking and reading. I enjoy serving food to the congregation in the gurdwara, our place of worship, and telling other children about my religion. I also like meditating in the morning before going to school.

In this book, four children share their experiences of the Sikh faith. It is important to remember that other Sikhs will have different opinions and experiences of their own faith.

A Sikh Life
Amrita's story

▲ *Closing my eyes, I meditate on the name of God.*

Akaalsimran says:
Guru Nanak is famous for saying "Ek Ongkar", which means God is one. This is the most important truth of the Sikh religion.

Sikhs believe that there is one God. We see God not as a person, but as a spiritual power in our hearts and minds. We believe that God should always be in our minds. In order to keep God in my mind, I often do Waheguru simran, which means meditating on God.

Karma

Sikhs believe that when we die, we are reborn into another life. The quality of this life depends on how well we have behaved in the previous life. We describe the negative and positive effects of our behaviour as **karma**. It is important to do positive things to create good karma. This means that we work hard to keep God in our minds, develop our personalities and reach the goals in our lives.

Helping others

We also aim to do good by helping other people. I try to do this by showing love and affection and sharing my things with those around me. Sikhs also help other people by means of **seva**. Seva means supporting those who are poorer or less fortunate than us. Usually, we perform seva at the gurdwara by giving clothes and medicines to needy people and by helping with their education. We try to treat all people equally, because we are all created by God and God is in everyone and everything.

A meal for everyone

One way in which I learn to serve others is by helping to make **langar**, the meal that we all eat after the service in the gurdwara. We serve langar to everyone who comes to the gurdwara, no matter which religion they follow or how rich or poor they are. We eat vegetables, rice, salad and a rice pudding called kheer.

▼ *We all eat the langar meal together after the service.*

The Gurus
Akaalsimran's story

▲ *In our gurdwara we sing many hymns that were written by Guru Nanak and the other gurus.*

Guru Nanak was the first Sikh guru and the founder of the Sikh religion. He lived in Talwandi, a village 65 kilometres west of Lahore, Pakistan.

Instructions from God
One day, Guru Nanak went to the river to bathe as usual. But he heard God calling to him and went into a forest on the other side of the river to get instructions from God. People thought he had drowned in the river, but after three days he returned.

Attracting followers
Guru Nanak was a spiritual person and believed deeply in God. He told everyone about his beliefs by preaching and by composing many hymns in praise of God, which inspired people to follow the Sikh religion.

10

The Anand Sahib

Guru Amar Das was the third of the Sikh gurus. He wrote a famous hymn called the *Anand Sahib* (the song of bliss) for the wedding of his daughter, Bibi Bhani, to Ram Das, who later became the fourth guru. We sing the *Anand Sahib* just before **Ardas**, at the end of services in the gurdwara.

The last guru

Guru Gobind Singh was the last human guru. His many achievements include winning battles against bullies, writing many hymns, founding the city of Anandpur and forming the **Khalsa** (see page 16–17). Before he died, he told people that they should take Guru Granth Sahib as their guru, bringing the line of human gurus to an end.

Guru Nanak was the founder of Sikhism. ▶

The Ten Gurus
Guru Nanak (1469–1539)
Guru Angad Dev (1504–1552)
Guru Amar Das (1479–1574)
Guru Ram Das (1534–1581)
Guru Arjan Dev (1563–1606)
Guru Hargobind (1595–1644)
Guru Har Rai (1630–1661)
Guru Har Krishan (1656–1664)
Guru Tegh Bahadur (1621–1675)
Guru Gobind Singh (1666–1708)

Sehaj says:
Guru Nanak followed God's path by doing good deeds and spreading the message of truth and equality.

Guru Granth Sahib
Sunny's story

◀ *We bow as Guru Granth Sahib is carried through the gurdwara.*

Akaalsimran says:
To show that the book should be the next guru, Guru Gobind Singh bowed before it, making his forehead touch the floor.

Guru Granth Sahib is the sacred book of the Sikh religion. We call it a guru because it is the living guru of the Sikhs. Its title means 'holy book' and it is also known as Adi Granth, which means 'sacred text'.

A collection of writings
The hymns in Guru Granth Sahib were written by the first five gurus (see page 11) and by some great Hindu and Muslim saints. The book contains these writings by both Hindus and Muslims to show that all beings are equal, regardless of colour, social status or religion.

The fifth guru, Guru Arjan Dev, collected these writings together in

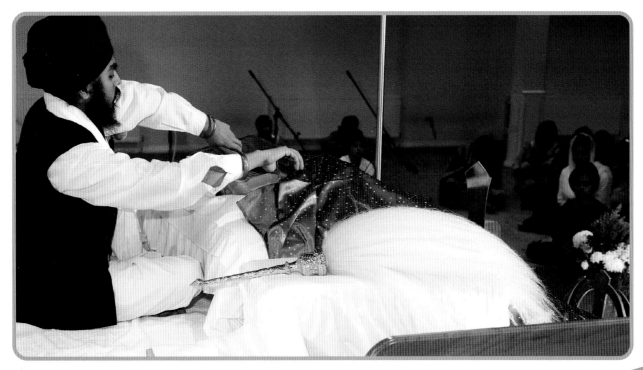

▲ *We listen carefully when the reading of Guru Granth Sahib begins.*

one book. He organised the writings under the original Ragas (or melodies) in which they were sung. Over the years, Sikhs have not changed the order of the writings in the text.

Respect for the book

Every gurdwara has a copy of the book. It is kept in a special place and we treat it with great respect. At the start of worship it is carried carefully to the main hall of the gurdwara and placed on a platform called the Manji Sahib ('Throne'). When not being read, the book is covered with a special cloth.

Sehaj says:
At our gurdwara the children do the Chhoti Ardas. This is the short prayer said when Guru Granth Sahib is put away for the evening.

Waving the **chauri** *over Guru* ▶
Granth Sahib is a sign of respect.

13

Prayer at Home
Sunny's story

▲ *When I pray I sit still and put my hands together.*

We believe that it is important to pray because it is a way of spending time with God and it guides us towards living a peaceful and meaningful life. Although we go to the gurdwara regularly, we do not have to go there to pray. Sikhs can also pray at home and my mum does so every day.

Beginning the day

Although Sikhs can pray at any time of the day, many believe that you should begin the day with prayers. My mum gets up early every day. She takes a shower then puts on a special dress and covers her head. Then she says her prayers using her prayer books.

◄ *My mum says her prayers every morning before she starts her day.*

Prayers for different times

We recite different prayers at different times of day. **Japji** is the morning prayer. We say it, together with the Mool Mantar, at the beginning of the day. Mool Mantar is the very first text in Guru Granth Sahib and it was written by Guru Nanak. After a hard day's work, we recite the evening prayer, Rehras, which brings back our energy. At bedtime, we recite a group of hymns from Guru Granth Sahib that are known as Sohila.

> *Akaalsimran says:*
> The Mool Mantar is important because it describes what God is like and what Guru Granth Sahib means to Sikhs.

▼ *Sometimes, my family gets together for a discussion about our faith.*

Joining the Khalsa
Sunny's story

▲ *Five Khalsa members gather round to mix sugar crystals and water to make amrit.*

To join the Khalsa, the community of Pure or baptised Sikhs, a person takes part in the amrit ceremony. We can do this as soon as we are old enough to understand the commitment we are making. Afterwards, we take a new name and wear the Five Ks.

The amrit ceremony
The ceremony takes place in the gurdwara. Five members of the Khalsa, standing for the original five members, the Panj Piyaras, must be present. They mix amrit by adding sugar to water and stir the mixture with a kirpan (short sword). When it is ready, the people

who are going to join the Khalsa drink some of the amrit from the bowl, before some of it is sprinkled on their hair and eyes.

Teaching about the religion

Each person who is joining the Khalsa then recites the Mool Mantar. This is one of our most important prayers because it shows what it means to be a Sikh. We read from Guru Granth Sahib and someone explains the importance of the ceremony and the rules of the Sikh religion.

Karah Parshad

At the end of the ceremony, everyone at the gurdwara eats Karah Parshad. This is a special sweet food made from a mixture of flour, sugar and ghee (clarified butter).

The founding of the Khalsa

One day, Guru Gobind Singh asked five people to volunteer to be beheaded. Five brave men came forward and the guru took them into a tent before coming out with a blood-stained sword. But then the five men came out of the tent alive. The guru called them the Five Beloved Ones, the first members of the Khalsa. He gave them their Sikh names and the Five Ks that became the uniform of the Sikhs.

> *Akaalsimran says:*
> When Guru Gobind Singh founded the Khalsa, he created a new race where everyone was equal.

◀ *Guru Granth Sahib open on the Manji Sahib ('Throne').*

The Five Ks
Sehaj's story

W hen Guru Gobind Singh founded the Khalsa, the community of initiated **Sikhs,** he told people to wear five things to show that they were Sikhs. These five things all have names beginning with the letter K and so are known as the Five Ks.

The meaning of the Five Ks

Kesh, uncut hair, is a gift from God and identifies us as Sikhs. The kara is a steel bracelet. Its perfect, circular shape reminds us of God and discourages us from doing wrong. The kirpan is a short sword, a symbol of protection to remind us to defend

Sunny says:
The Khalsa is the name for the pure Sikhs who have had their amrit ceremony. When I have my amrit ceremony, I will wear the Five Ks.

▲ *This is me at our gurdwara. Sikh males normally cover their hair with a turban.*

those who are weaker than us. The kangha is a comb that we use to keep our hair tidy and stands for cleanliness. The kacha are shorts, worn as undergarments, as a symbol of chastity.

The turban

In addition to the Five Ks, we wear a turban. The turban is important to Sikhs because it covers our long hair and is also a sign of our pride and dignity.

Sikh names

Guru Gobind Singh also told Sikhs to take special names to show that they were members of the Sikh community. Sikh men have the name Singh, which means lion and Sikh women are called **Kaur**, which means princess.

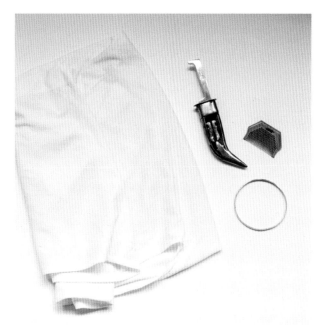

▲ *The kacha, kirpan, kara and kangha are four of the Five Ks.*

Kesh, uncut hair, is the first K ▶ and the most important one.

19

The Gurdwara
Amrita's story

▲ *I am reciting a poem in the gurdwara. My grandmother is playing the harmonium and my father and grandfather are sitting behind me.*

Our gurdwara has a large central dome and smaller domes around the sides. Like most gurdwaras, it has four doors, to show that it is open to all people. A saffron **flag**, called the Nishan Sahib, flies in front of the building to show that it is a gurdwara.

This is the gurdwara where I worship. ▶

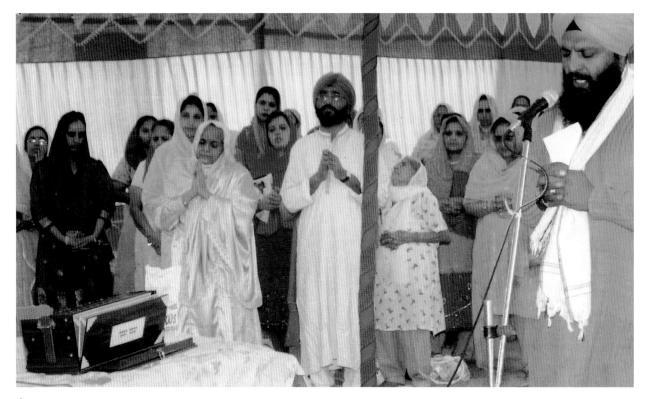

▲ *At the end of our worship we stand for the prayer called Ardas. We stand up with our hands folded together facing Guru Granth Sahib while we think about God.*

Going to the gurdwara

When I enter the gurdwara I take off my shoes, wash my hands and feet, cover my head and bow down. Our worship in the gurdwara includes singing, prayer, reading and meditation. I learn about serving others, being honest, being a proud Sikh and respecting all religions.

Sehaj says:
I love going to the gurdwara because I feel close to God. I go with my family every Friday and Saturday.

Housing the book

Inside the gurdwara there are no pictures or statues because our religion is not based on images, but on the teachings of Guru Granth Sahib, which shows us the right path to take through life. Guru Granth Sahib is housed in the gurdwara like a king on his throne. The place where the book is housed is kept clean and the book is laid on clean cushions and covered with beautiful, colourful cloths called **rumalas**.

▲ *I do service to Guru Granth Sahib by waving the chauri.*

Doing service to the holy book

We respect the holy book as the guru and king who presides over the 'darbar' or congregation at the gurdwara. To show our devotion to the book we do service to the guru by using a fan or fly whisk called a chauri. This is a custom that goes back to ancient times, when servants used to keep kings or noblemen cool and comfortable by waving a fan or whisk above their heads. Any member of the congregation is allowed to serve the guru in this way.

Favourite Festivals
Sehaj's story

▲ I play tabla during a Gurpurb.

Sunny says:
On Guru Nanak's birthday we decorate our gurdwara with flowers, lights, flags and banners.

One of the most important dates in our year is the birthday of Guru Nanak. This is one of the Gurpurbs – festivals that are linked to the lives of the gurus. I enjoy the Gurpurbs because our gurdwara is beautifully decorated and we dress in our best clothes to go to the services.

The Akhand Path
We celebrate the Gurpurbs with an **Akhand Path**, a continuous reading out loud, from beginning to end, of Guru Granth Sahib. The reading takes place at our gurdwara. The Akhand Path begins in the morning and continues for 48 hours until the day of the Gurpurb itself. Many members of the congregation take part in the reading. Usually each person reads for about an hour, although some people read for about two hours.

23

Things to do

I enjoy some of the other celebrations that take place at our gurdwara during the Gurpurbs. There are classes in Punjabi and Sikh history and soccer tournaments for children, which are a lot of fun. Our congregation does a sponsored walk to raise money for charity and I also take part in the speech competitions that take place every year.

Vaisakhi

We celebrate the festival of **Vaisakhi** in the month of April. Vaisakhi is the anniversary of the time when Guru Gobind Singh founded the Khalsa. It is a time when we offer special devotion to God. Because this festival celebrates the Khalsa, this is the day on which many people have their amrit ceremony and become Khalsa members (see page 16–17) .

▲ *This picture shows me giving a speech at our gurdwara. I was really pleased when I won a prize for this speech.*

At the gurdwara

On Vaisakhi we put up saffron and blue decorations in our gurdwara – these colours symbolise the Khalsa. On the day of the festival, we put on our best white or blue turbans and go to the gurdwara for a special service with music and hymn-singing. After worship there is a special ceremony called Nishan Sahib Sewa. During this ceremony, the Nishan Sahib is renewed. This is when we replace the old flag with a new one.

This is the Nishan Sahib, the flag raised ▶
outside our gurdwara that we renew at the
festival of Vaisakhi.

The procession

We also celebrate Vaisakhi with a special procession through the streets. Five men, representing the first members of the Khalsa or Five Beloved Ones, lead the procession. Guru Granth Sahib is also brought out to join the procession. The book is carried carefully and with great respect. It is placed on a platform on top of a beautifully decorated truck.

Sunny says:
Before the procession we sing hymns. Then we follow the Five Beloved Ones through the town, eating special foods and Indian sweets on the way.

◀ *Several members of my family took part in the procession at Vaisakhi. Here my brother Tejasvir and my father are taking part in kirtan (a kind of chanting that forms part of Sikh worship) during the procession.*

A New Baby
Akaalsimran's story

"

▲ *My name means Angel of Eternal Meditation.*

The Mool Mantar
This is one English translation of the Mool Mantar:
There is only one God. Truth is his name. He is the creator. He is without fear. He is without hatred. He is beyond time. He is beyond birth and death. He is self-existent. He is realised by the grace of the Guru.

When a new baby is born into a Sikh family, the child's parents follow the instructions for ceremonies in the Sikh Rahit Maryada (Sikh Code of Conduct). I have no younger brothers or sisters, but my parents have told me what they did when I was born.

Finding a name

When I was born, my mother whispered the words of the prayer called the Mool Mantar into my ear. Later, while my mum was still in hospital after I was born, my dad took my brother, grandparents, uncles and aunties to the gurdwara. After a special Ardas (prayer) the **giani** opened Guru Granth Sahib at random and read the first verse from the left-hand page. He then told my dad the first letter of this verse, which was the letter A. My parents therefore chose a name beginning with A, Akaalsimran. My full name means Angel of Eternal Meditation. My mum explains that my name is my destiny and that I have a responsibility to fulfil it. It sounds difficult, but I pray that I will achieve it.

Sharing amrit

Then, 40 days later, my mum took me to the gurdwara for the first time to take part in the ceremony called Janam Sanskar. When we arrived at the gurdwara, my mum sat in front of Guru Granth Sahib. The giani began by making amrit, by adding some cubes of sugar to a small iron bowl filled with water. He stirred the water and sugar with a small kirpan while reciting the first five verses of the Japji, the first prayer of Guru Granth Sahib. Then he sprinkled the mixture on my face and gave my mother the rest to drink. She shared some of the mixture with my dad and my older brother.

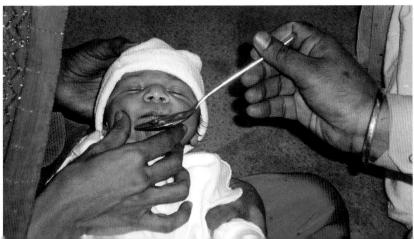

◀ *These pictures are from the Janam Sanskar ceremony of a friend.*
Top left – stirring the amrit.
Above – sharing the amrit.
Bottom left – sprinkling the amrit onto the baby.

27

Glossary

Akhand Path A complete reading out loud of Guru Granth Sahib.

amrit Holy water, sweetened with sugar and used in rituals, including the ceremony (often called the amrit ceremony) that admits people into the Khalsa.

Ardas The special prayer that ends services in the gurdwara.

chauri A whisk that is waved over Guru Granth Sahib as a mark of respect.

community A group of people living together or sharing the same beliefs or culture.

Five Ks The five items, all with names that begin with the letter K, worn by Sikhs as symbols of their faith.

giani A person who is deeply knowledgeable about Sikh teachings and scriptures.

gurdwara The building where a copy of Guru Granth Sahib is properly housed. Sikhs worship together in a gurdwara.

Gurpurbs Festivals that commemorate the birth or death of one of the gurus.

guru One of the ten people who led the early Sikhs. The title guru is also given to the sacred text, Guru Granth Sahib.

Guru Granth Sahib The Sikh sacred book; also known as Adi Granth.

Harmandir The Golden Temple at Amritsar.

initiated The term used to describe someone who has been through a ritual, such as the amrit ceremony, to gain entry into the religious community.

Japji The hymn written by Guru Nanak at the beginning of Guru Granth Sahib.

karma The teaching that all our actions have effects or consequences, and that these consequences affect our happiness day by day and in our future lives.

Kaur The name given to all female Sikhs, which means princess.

Khalsa The community of Sikhs that has been through the amrit ceremony and that shows its commitment to the Sikh religion by wearing the Five Ks.

langar The vegetarian meal eaten together by the congregation at the gurdwara.

Nishan Sahib The saffron flag that flies outside a gurdwara.

Punjab The area on the borders of India and Pakistan where Sikhism began and where many Sikhs still live.

rumalas The beautiful cloths that cover Guru Granth Sahib.

saffron An orange colour.

seva Actions such as helping others, giving to the poor and helping in the gurdwara.

Singh The name given to all male Sikhs, which means lion.

tikkas A traditional form of Indian jewellery that is worn hanging from the parting of the hair to the centre of the forehead.

Vaisakhi The spring festival that takes place in April and marks the foundation of the Khalsa by Guru Gobind Singh.

Further Information

Websites

BBC Religion and Ethics
www.bbc.co.uk/religion/religions/sikhism

Religion Facts
www.religionfacts.com/sikhism/index.htm

Sikhism: Thy Name is Love and Sacrifice
www.srigurugranthsahib.org/main.htm

SikhiWiki: Free Sikh Encyclopedia
sikhiwiki.com/index.php/Main_Page

Note to parents and teachers: Every effort has been made by the Publishers to ensure that these websites are suitable for children, that they are of the highest educational value, and that they contain no inappropriate or offensive material. However, because of the nature of the Internet, it is impossible to guarantee that the contents of these sites will not be altered. We strongly advise that Internet access is supervised by a responsible adult.

The Sikh Year

The Sikh religious year is marked by the Gurpurbs, the festivals commemorating events in the lives of the gurus, and other festivals, such as Sikh Diwali and Vaisakhi. With the exception of Vaisakhi, the festivals are held at specific points in the Sikh calendar, so that they occur on different dates in the western months.

Month of Chet (February/March)
Hola Mohalla

A festival commemorating a time in the early history of Sikhism when Sikh men gathered to train in the martial arts so that they could defend themselves.

13 April (occasionally 14 April)
Vaisakhi

The Punjabi New Year festival also marks the occasion when Guru Gobind Singh founded the Khalsa. It is the only Sikh festival that is held on the same date in the western calendar each year (except for once every 36 years, when it is held on 14 April).

30

Month of Jaith (May/June)
Martyrdom of Guru Arjan

Guru Arjan was tortured by enemies and died in 1606, staying true to his beliefs. When he was tortured in the hot month of June he was not allowed to drink anything, so on this day Sikhs give drinks to passers-by to quench their thirst and as a reminder of the way their guru suffered.

Month of Katik (October/November)
Sikh Diwali in honour of Guru Hargobind

Diwali was originally the Hindu festival of lights. Like Hindus, Sikhs light lamps at Diwali, but in addition they commemorate Guru Hargobind. Sikhs celebrate with gifts of sweets and displays of fireworks at the Golden Temple.

Month of Katik (October/November)
Birthday of Guru Nanak

Games, fairs and fêtes mark the three-day commemoration of Guru Nanak, which is a time both of celebration and solemn reflection.

Month of Poh (November/December)
Martyrdom of Guru Tegh Bahadur

Guru Tegh Bahadur was killed because he stood for the right of all people to practice their religion.

Month of Magh (December/January)
Birthday of Guru Gobind Singh

After the birthday of Guru Nanak, this commemoration of the founder of the Khalsa is the most important of the Gurpurbs and it is celebrated by Sikhs worldwide.

Index